The Book of Mankey

The Book of Mankey

Richard Pierce

Cooper Dillon

Acknowledgments

I would like to thank Bill Wenthe, my dissertation advisor at Texas Tech University, for all his time, help, friendship, and belief in me. I would also like to thank the following for all their help and support: Ma, Dad, Marc Gartler, Nathan Anderson, Lee McCarthy, Texas Tech University, Brent Newsom, Adam Houle, Curtis Bauer, John Poch, Jackie Kolosov, William Wilson, Jimmy Kinnon, Dr. Robert Smith, and all my fellowship friends.

Most of all I thank the Holy Trinity. To thee, O Lord.

Thank you to the following journals, where versions of the following poems have appeared, sometimes under different titles:
    "*Fall*": *New South*
    "Ruler of the Skies' Diorama," "Coming To," and "Exhausted, Mankey Sleeps, Dreams He's His Dead Dog, Mitch": *Birmingham Poetry Review*
    "Penny Livingston and the Red-Spotted Newt": *Ninth Letter*
    "Evening Midway": *Relief*
    "Ride the Galaxy Ferris": *Poet Lore*
"Moonlit" contains a passage translated from "The Seafarer," from the *Exeter Book*.

The Book of Mankey
Copyright © 2015 by Richard Pierce
All rights reserved
First edition
Cooper Dillon Books
San Diego, California
CooperDillon.com

Cover Art & Design: Max Xiantu

ISBN-10: 0-9841928-9-1
ISBN-13: 978-0-9841928-9-2

Printed in the United States

Table of Contents

Fall	1
Moonlit	3
"Ruler Of The Skies" Diorama	5
1969 Stingray Corvette	7
Coming To	8
Sunny Hollow, #3	10
Exhausted, Mankey Sleeps, Dreams He's His Dead Dog, Mitch	12
Oil Creek	13
Opal Menninger	15
Sunken Church In Kinzua Reservoir	18
Hugh Livingston, Honeydipper	20
Why the Singing Girl He Saw on the Bicycle Swerved	23
Penny Livingston and the Red-Spotted Newt	25
Karma	27
Kinzua Railroad Bridge, 301½ Feet High	28
Evening Midway	29
Last Night	30
Bearly	31
Ride the Galaxy Ferris	33

… because time and chance happen to them all.

Ecclesiastes 9:11

Fall

*That day the baby died and killed my wife,
the hills were blood and rotting fruit, smeared
across the windshield. My silver Mustang veered
through cliff-hung curves above the river; life
was through with me and I was through with life—
I knew a spot. The only thing I feared
was that I'd burn before I died. It's weird
the things you sometimes think ... my baby, my wife.*

*I gunned it through the final curve—a flare
shot pink. I clenched my teeth and downshifted—
an accident. No:—just a flat. That family:
the serious man was crouched beside the spare;
the wife enjoyed the view—she turned, lifted
the daughter's tiny arm and waved at me.*

Ten years later.

Moonlit

Mankey, dizzy with a migraine,
kneels in his golf shirt
at the edge of a swamp.

In the black leather passenger seat,
the pistol and a brass
train-wreck of bullets.

Beneath the dingy dome light,
words in a book throb, trapped
by frantic gray pencil swirls
and stranded on the floorboard:

> *He who lives on land most pleasantly,*
> *such a man cannot know how I,*
> *a wanderer without beloved kinsmen,*
> *have dwelt the ice-cold seaways of winter,*
> *covered by icicles and full of sorrows.*

Thirsty, he tries to clear away
the green slime
from the reflection of his face,
but each attempt
eddies in more algae.
        He dips a cupped hand—
gags at the taste.

The far shore sways
and heaves; beyond, a field
glows dully.

When he starts across, sludge
takes one of his sneakers.

He whispers: *Anything!*
I'll do anything!

A frog stomach plops.

"Ruler Of The Skies" Diorama

Headquarters, Enchanted Mountains State Park

The eagle is elegant
in its dive, despite
the dusty, unkempt
feathers of its head
and the silver glint
of piano wire.

A lacquered trout
stuck on a stick
rises to a green lacewing.

Mud-fragrant, Mankey
sips coffee on the bench.

I know how you feel.
You're just going along
minding your business—
wham!—some goon's got you
by the neck.

He approaches
the smudged window.

But your friends,
if you have any, get to float along
like those minnows there by the weeds,
eating their steaks probably,
watching TV ...

He strikes the pane
with his palm—

the apparent malice
of the eagle's eye
is only indifferent glass.

1969 Stingray Corvette

A few hours later. Nearly dawn.

A swerving canary blur,
the Stingray sprints along the river.

Fixed inside
by the incantation of the drive,
Mankey feels the world expand, clarified
by its reduction to asphalt, wheels,
orange-needle dials, and the trees
swiftly passing.

The challenge of the road's many curves,
the rises, the falls met with mastery unite
moment and movement
and finally released his mind dissolves
into brake and steer, gas and gear.

Where would he be without
such perfect command,
the power and control
of this bellowing outpost?

Coming To

Les Mankey, D.D.S. Afternoon.

                You think
some things about yourself will never change,
but then you wake up thirsty, half-dead
inside some shack that smells like fish, the door
kicked in, a loaded pistol in your hand.
But isn't that the way your world explodes?
Thursday night had seemed the same as any.
I wax my car and watch a little ball,
but then I can't find the phone and Mitch
takes off when I let him out. I call and whistle,
wait at the door. He finally comes blasting across
the Johnson's lawn and leaps, taking me down.
It doesn't make a bit of sense. Mitch's
a good boy, lazy, doesn't even bark
at cars, but there we are, locked and rolling,
lamps toppling, spit flying, curtains tear, skin tears—
a slipper, the paper—I grope around for something—
anything—and whack his head with all I got
and eighty pounds of limp retriever thuds
across my chest. My hand begins to ring—
I'd poached ol' Mitch by cordless telephone.
Hello there, sir. And how are you today.
Wonderful. *Great. I have some news for you.
But first, I need to check—Dr. Mankey,
correct?* Yes. *Are you sitting down? You should.*
Yes. *Well, you will be glad to know that no one
was hurt.* Who is this? *Sorry—Chief McGruder,
the Orin Fire Department. You did a root
canal on me a few years back, turned out
just fine. No pain since. Anyway doc, there's been
an accident—a fire. Now like I said, nobody
was injured, but it spread too fast.* What?

Yes, it's your office, sir—a total loss.
I took a breath and let it out. It sounded odd: long
and loud—like that was all I still had left,
like that was all I was—a naked, breathing
thing—like that was all I ever was.
                              And then
I woke up here, the night just gone—a blur.
Jesus. What can I do? First, Mitch. The office.
                                        God,
I know You're there. Will You—*I know you're there?*
That's what Sheila said about getting pregnant at her age.
I'm sick of this shit. What did I do to piss
you off? I feel like that guy you kicked around,
that famous one—his name—it starts with J,
I think—the one you fed to the whale
after you killed his kids, his wife, and donkeys.
So I'm just sitting there quietly minding my business,
I'm watching a little golf and then—Jabonah!
I knew it. That's him. I knew it started with J.
Jabonah—You screwed him too, didn't you?
And now it's my turn again, I guess. It's like
you think that you're the Boss and everything
and everyone is yours. Well, it isn't—
I'll tell you that right now. I'm not.

Sunny Hollow, #3

A short time later.

From the shade
of the cabin porch,
Mankey looks up
at the sparkling parade
of foliage and light.

With the pistol's barrel,
he scratches the back of his neck,
looks down at the bullet
on the railing. A slight

rustle of leaves from the circled
stones of the fire ring:
a chipmunk peeks.

Mankey fills the chamber,
places muzzle to temple.

—There, at eye level,
clinging to the green porch post,
the crusted gold
of a cicada husk.

Where was it now,
this changed riser?

What wings? What sights?

And what could they matter,
those cramped years
of claustrophobic dark
spent clawing through the hard earth,
gnawing bitter roots
for what juice they held?

Exhausted, Mankey Sleeps, Dreams He's His Dead Dog, Mitch

Muzzled Mitch moans.
Deeper down he dug.
The dirt did not boon bones.
The hole has grown.
He thought himself wily while he went,
never doubting, nor noticing his maw.
Then he saw. Now his nose
sticks stupid up—the walls
too tall to crawl.
He thought that there
were bones beneath,
but now he knows. Night nears.

Far from fair:
someone should have been above
to hear him jump or claw.
For hours he thought
master might.
Now he knows.
Colder, colder, grows the night.
His fur failing, down he lies.
Lost, he moans. Now
he knows.

Oil Creek

Behind Park Headquarters. Mankey eats a little.

Midstream, the hippie bows his head
over a book of flies.

Mankey chuckles to himself
at the picnic table, nurses
a Rocky Road sugar cone.

Twenty minutes
and that crackpot still believes
there's something alive in there.

Can't he see
the candy-colored cans along the shore,
the sunken washing machine?

Can't he hear that jagged
rasp of grocery sack
tangled in the branches?

The neon line loads, unfurls.
Feather and fur
drift along overhung scrub.

He lashes the line again.

Unperturbed, the fly,
tethered to invisible leader,
rides the slight, almost indiscernible
ripple of the surface.

Another cast, same spot.

Mankey spins the cold
against his tongue.

When he looks back,
the hippie's rod is raised.
He strips taut line:

no splash or ripple.

What? Can't he even tell
when he's snagged
a branch or a boot?

What is this guy?
A fisher of trash?

Mankey crunches the cone.

The hippie kneels down, raises up
a brown trout to his face.

He points and waves to Mankey,
sets the fish free.

Opal Menninger

What's that, dear? Can you speak up?
Oh, Lord. I see. So the keys to your motor vehicle
are now, what was that? Oh yes,
you think you dropped them earlier in,
in what? I see. So the keys to your vehicle
are now dropped in the outhouse outside the store?
Well now. It seems to me we should
perhaps endeavor to try to locate a solution
to this current problem we are now facing.
Are you ok? Your face looks a little red-hued,
beetish even. I see. Only a sunburn.
Well, it didn't look red a moment ago in the past,
but who knows with the way the sky is these days,
what with the ozone and all? Why I remember
when I was a young lady back in glorious Tennessee,
we never once worried—Pardon? Yes, of course. Your keys.
Well, I wonder …
It seems we should perhaps endeavor to—
Well now. There's no need to be impatient. I am only attempting,
in your most disgruntled and so sadly bereaved state,
to alleviate your pain by helping you to … What was it?
Yes. Yes, of course. Your keys. I am only attempting
to help you in your most unfortunate
and currently unlucky state to locate your keys.
Now let's see. Yes, I have a feeling I may need
to examine our daily—yes, here we are.
The calendar … Well, this won't exactly
eradicate your bereavement and I am sure
you are more than cognizant of the glorious events
scheduled to transpire this very night and into the weekend,
but here is a—Hold your tongue, boy!
Didn't your mother never teach you

the Good Book says it is most rude
to interrupt a lady, especially when she is embarking upon
a most heartfelt transmission of a genuine handmade
promotional Xeroxed announcement flyer,
the contents of which will no doubt brighten
and alleviate some of the unfortunateness
of the unlucky situation you currently face. Now,
as I was saying, before I was so impertinently interrupted
in a way most unbecoming of a young man
of an obviously low-cultured heathen heritage
that doesn't even properly appreciate the sweetly value
of patience, here is the heartfelt announcement flyer
for this weekend's carnival. Pardon? Oh yes,
the calendar. I knew there was something. It seems here
according to this accurate listing of daily tasks
that our local honeydipper—a fascinating fellow really,
abreast of all the latest developments
in present-day computer recreations—
was scheduled to drain our store outhouse,
in addition to and including those
along the Red Belly Slider camping trail.
Indeed, he was scheduled to empty them all
into his honey retrieval and transportation vehicle
this very morning, a vehicle which I can now
clearly remembrance witnessing
shortly after you acquired your sugared cone.
I am sorry, sir, but I presently fear
and must sadly confess
its rather large cylindrical receptacle
may now be the location of the aforementioned keys
to your said motor vehicle. You truly are lucky:
he lives only right outside the park, and if you will wait
another moment or two, I will return to our backroom
and endeavor to locate his telephone number.
Oh dear! Your face, it's turned again—
even redder than before! Sweet Jesus

and Stonewall's men! It's worse
than I originally imagined! We must act fastly
and without a moment's hesitation.
Wait right here, while I radio our park ranger, Daisy Lamb,
a goodly Christian woman, who will pray you
through this currently perilous bedevilment plaguing your—
What? Oh, about four miles past the lake—.
But—Well, I suppose you could walk to his residence,
but with the current state of your skin, the sun, and your very soul
I would sincerely implore and recommend you—Very well.

Sunken Church In Kinzua Reservoir

Lt. Daisy Lamb, Park Ranger

There it is. My joy
returns whenever I see
the pale, drowned steeple
and my dive lamp scans
spongy shingles to find my
neat, pry-barred portal.

Inside, I corkscrew
round the pulpit, swim a slow
lap or two above
the dark pews, always checking—
I don't know why—the black lock
on the double doors.

Then, up to the high
giant waterlogged cross, which,
rough-hewn and stained, hangs,
chained to the rafters,
the place I keep the dishrag
I use to clean You.

This window captures
You best, Lord. Your eyes, they look
the most serious,
ignoring the boy
and grimy girl who compete
for your attention.

Her shabby flowers
are nothing to you. You look
through her, past the stone
palazzo arches
to the emerald hills which look
local to the park.

It just warms my heart
knowing You accept my prayer.
I only wish I
could be sure You hear
Hoppler, that liberal, doe-eyed
dope of a reverend.

Forgive me. Please help
him not forget that perfect,
glorious truth that
gives Your life, works, love
all the meaning they possess.
Let him remember

Hell. May he cherish
it and never forget or
try to do away
with it, that great proof
of Your infinitely un-
conditional love.

Hugh Livingston, Honeydipper

The barn behind Hugh's house

Hey, give me a minute, will you? Ain't you never seen nobody
hot on the heels of a Frogger record score before?
Sorry, but you ain't getting me this time semis.
I don't care how many eighteen wheels you got,
I'm nimble, light on my toes, just plain way too much frog
for you to handle or for you to—Keep it down, jackass!
I need to concen—Sonuvabitch! Look what you made me do!
Dip me in shit and call me a pickle! Gotdamnit!
Well, speak up already.
What, cat got your tongue all a sudden? Come on.
—*Oh,* you need my help. A customer?
Well, why didn't you say so in the first place? Come on in.
Put her there, pal. Honey Hugh's the name
and sucking clean your septic tank's my game.
If you got problems with your tank or your can,
I'm definitely your man. So what can I do you for?
Come again? You think your keys got sucked up into my truck?
—Oh, that's right. That biddy from the park headquarters called,
said something 'bout you might be stopping by.
Funny, you don't look that mean or sunburned to me …
Anyway, I ain't drained my truck yet. You'll have to come back
later—Sunday maybe or Monday.
So what kind of car is it? *'69 Corrrvette!* No shit!
You feeling alright, friend? You look like somebody just died.
It never gets easy, does it? —Stuff not going your way.
I've lost my keys myself, one time in this tank
I was dipping way up on Nichols Run. *That* wasn't pretty.
You ever seen the people up there? Man, talk about rednecks.
Anyway, far as I can tell, plenty of shit in this world:
we're in it—born in it—ain't no getting out of it.
Even if you think you're smart or into that boo-hiss medication
or whatever the hell that stuff is called. I had this worker once—

           a college boy—Hoppler—
used to do that crap every morning. I'd be getting the rig ready
and he'd be in the back shed on a gotdamn pillow—ha! I'd tell
           him,
You're still a honeydipper, son, and the smell of your boots
ain't changed none—no matter what cloud your head's in.
Who in the hell never learned nothing anyhow by staring at a
           wall
with your legs all pretzeled-up Indian-style?
I'll tell you—nobody. I ain't dumb, you know—
but don't ask him. He knew it all of course.
But that's how it is. When I was young I thought, I'm strong
and the whole world's just there jugs-up for the humpin'.
I had my way a little while—still do at times—I mean, take a
           look around—
but after you get kicked off enough many times you think,
I got it: I just need to get over the fact that don't nothing
always go your way. It makes sense, but every time
it's just as bad. And you think, But I thought I'd get good at this.
Well, ain't no getting good. They used to call it wisdom, I think,
           but there ain't no wisdom
except knowing you ain't never gonna be wise
and you eventually gonna get kicked in the teeth again—
every time—ain't no way around it—and it always hurts the same.
Come again? "Perspective" and "habits of thought"
have something do with it? Sounds like a load of yuppie bullshit,
if you ask me. Come here, let me knee you in the nads
and then you can show me how you perspective yourself outta
           that one.
Relax. You ain't gotta backpedal. I'm just making a point.
You just go ahead and keep trying to pick the lock
on the universe's secret dungeon, I'd rather save my breath
and play a little Space Invaders. That's why I got this game room.
Go ahead, take a look around. That's right, read 'em and weep.
One of the best collections you'll ever see.
I got most all the classics, whatever your flavor:

Pac-Man, Donkey Kong, Ms. Pac-Man—regular
and table-top—that one's rare—I think—Dig-Dug, Missile Command,
Centipede, Q★Bert, Berzerk,—and ...
well, Frogger and Space Invaders of course. Yep,
I keep these games going best I can, and I guess they do the same for me.
Sure, they fritz out pretty regular and a lot of 'em
are still basket cases—gutted and in need of work—
but I always got at least a few of 'em up and running.
I been working on that Frogger for something like a few months.
Finally got it cranking this afternoon before you showed up.
Like I said, ain't no getting good: best you can hope for's
a little fun and distraction. That's what I always tell my little girl.
I mean, don't you think after all them years
somebody woulda found the key for lasting happiness if it existed?
The way I figured it, we just ain't wired for it—
just like Darlin said. Incapable.
That's what I tried telling that Hoppler over and over. It ain't in your—
what is it?—D.M.A.? It just ain't there, just like Darlin said.
Come on. You know. Darlin—
that famous scientologist that talked about them turtle and frog's
    revolution.
Say there's a cave man in the olden days just laying around,
but he starts to liking it too much. You know what happens next?
I'll tell you, someone comes and bonks your head
and after that your girl and when you wake up you know better
than go and do something stupid like going and getting comfy or
    satisfied
because in the end you know it will kill you. Well, maybe not so much
    today.
I mean, nothing wrong with Q★Bert and a few beers—
that's what I'm looking at tonight if I can get the damn thing running—
beats staring at a wall, wouldn't you think—
but overall that train's been on that track a whole lotta years—
millenemas, in fact. Millenemas. And it's probably supposed to be.
You can't expect it to turn on a dime.
Last I checked, don't many locomotives pull u-ies.

Why the Singing Girl He Saw on the Bicycle Swerved

At first Mankey thought
the roadkill frogs were coins
smudged with blood,

but then he realized
the unlikelihood of that.

It makes no sense,
he knows, to care about them,
but for the last mile or so

the pain has swollen,
while their unseen lives
flickered in his mind.

He saw the gelatinous bulbs
pulse and split.

He was there
as the larvae wriggled in ponds
and inch-deep algae flats—

even the temporary lake
of a forgotten spade.

The tail vanished,
the lungs deepened—they were his—
as the eyes bulged toward a life
sometimes lived on land,

and he no sooner nudged
the shore's indecipherable grassy maze,

when the electric-twitch
of dental floss tendons flashed
his thimble-weight into flight.

Strange things happen.
He is one of them.

He weeps for all their beautiful,
useless lives.

Penny Livingston and the Red-Spotted Newt

Aw. Thank you for asking. I'm okay. I hope you don't
mind me lifting your rocks—or you.
I wanted to talk about
something. Sometimes I feel so strange,
and I just can't figure it out.
It's like—a mystery. Like someone quiet's next to me.

Daddy was with his games (like always) and couldn't talk.
He said there ain't nothing you can't see
and that it's only fun
I'm feeling and that fun's the greatest thing
since spliced bread. I like the sun—
it's awesome—but didn't say. Here, Newty, you can sit on my
          shoulder.

I'm not sure, but I don't think the feeling's fun.
It's not the same as when you get
a yellow birthday cake
and presents. It's better. It's not like that
because you aren't afraid
for when your friends go home. It's like they stay inside you.

And I think he's maybe wrong about invisible things.
I've never seen a ghost before,
but some people do. You can't
see what happens in a microwave,
but popcorn can. It dances
happy—pop-pop-pop—because the electricity tickles it.

You might be right. Maybe the world *is* a giant
microwave. The feeling does make me
want to dance and my belly
feels so full, so warm and nice—
like after big spaghetti.
I like them noodles a lot, Newty. They make good friends.

Karma

Les Mankey, D.D.S., Dusk approaching.

For how many years have I alone and without
a bit of recognition whistled my way
into the room and offered my hand with a smile.
Every time, regardless of how I felt. Maybe
the patients weren't that afraid. But still, it mattered—
it must: I had a choice and I chose good.
I know it's wrong, but something in me cries,
Good begets good. Or should. Maybe I've had
my share: food, water, work, a place to live,
cars, golf; that's more than half the world can claim.
But what about all the help I gave?
How many mumbling people have called me at dawn
exhausted, gnashed to bits by the sleepless jaws
of tooth-pain? How many hours have I relieved
of agony? Six months? A year? Five? At least
a week or two. And what has it got me? Nothing.
Not a damn thing. I know it's childish to think
the world behaves like a coin machine.
It doesn't just comply—kerplunk—and drop
your demands instantly and in proportion to
the tinny mites of righteousness you slide
into the slot. The tastier fluff, whatever
you really want, stays locked inside: the Good
and Plenty, the Chuckles, and Lays. It isn't right…
Sure, I've had my health and quiet, but what is quiet
except a chance to really hear your pain.
I guess I should include family and love,
although they never seem enough—but none
of it ever does. Or not for very long.

Kinzua Railroad Bridge, 301½ Feet High

Les Mankey, D.D.S.

The moon's a grimy egg tonight. Nailed
to black, it leaks its curdled light. Below,
where the river glints, the gorge looks full of bones.
That sunny day when Armstrong made *his* leap
we cheered and ate marshmallows. I'd own the moon
by the time I was thirty, thirty-two. Bored
with all the Super Bowls and World Series—
winning would fizzle after the first few times—
I'd turn to wider fields: real estate,
then space—and finally both: a space hotel
for all my fans, complete with eighteen holes.
Eventually I lowered my head and ran,
adult enough to see I'd never fly.
The future glittered its American shine—
success and love in a picket fence—happiness—
mine all mine as long as I tried. But still
I lied. I see it now: I've lived my life
between the iron rails of what you want
and what you get. Except in that distant point
your mind misreads, they never meet. The two
that cross are you and death. That train takes all.

Evening Midway

The Reverend Brooks Hoppler

What except mercy
could create   the possibility

of onion rings stacked   ten high on sticks

foot-long dogs   on toasted buns
with neon relish   and bitter brown
squiggles of mustard

jumbo rainbow   two-hand sno-cones

white-hot atomic   pinstriped cinnamon taffy

chocolate-dipped   sprinkle or walnut rolled
frozen bananas

turkey legs   funnel cake   lemonade ...

What except   some divine perverse
design to please   could allow these
ordinary, intense   obscenities of grace?

Last Night

Les Mankey, D.D.S.

I would have sworn it would be my last.
Why else would I have climbed on the trestle?
Suspended on that timber, I saw the truth.
The distant hills, a stack of varied black;
below, bone-cold, the crumpled river flowed.
When I closed my eyes to take my quiet
final step, a tremor hummed into my legs
and the night around me seemed to sigh. I turned.
Sustained, faint at first, the sound grew stern
and spun into a twisted iron scream
but still it didn't hit me till I saw
the light explode in a brassy blast of trumpets.
A train approaching through a moment's eternity.
Stranded, I stared into my heart—drank deep
the rage of that bitter sponge. I stared and stared
but must've run. Face-first on the ballast stones,
the flashing crash of the passing wail crushed me
like a falling wall. Battered, buried, it seemed
two days of strangled dark before I breathed.
I stood and checked: alive. My hands bled red.
Today, the trees burn blue, pierced by light.

Bearly

Les Mankey, D.D.S. naps in his cabin and dreams.

1.
Brown-furred and burly,
ears strained for the strain
the stingered ones sing,
Mankey lumbers along a log,
hunting for honey.
Earlier he heard
a bee bumble its boozy
black-striped buzz and mumble
its yellow way away.
Now the sun slings hot silver.
Huffing hard
through pines, he pines.

2.
Weeks of wandering and damn it
later, still he hankers.
Drizzling his dreams,
the gaudy gold oozes
until he wakes whimpering—When?
He's never had such honey-hunger.
Last time it left,
he thinks. Then, like light
Heaven-hung, that high hive.
Mankey hurries and hugs
the trunk, tremors it free.
Cross-leggéd, cradling
that pummeled piñata of perfect,
at long last, he daubs a paw
and downs it, undaunted by bees.
Clear tears blubber and bubble.
Such sweetness.

Ride the Galaxy Ferris

Cresting above
the Day-Glo alleys of the midway,
lean forward.

Nothing will
ultimately come of this:

the structure simply spins
in the dark, but tonight,

you're glad to be aboard.

The final passengers loaded,
the wheel runs freely—

it all combines in a seamless
shifting perspective:

tents and vendors, glittering
pirate ship, the car's gentle sway;
screams, laughs, the packs and pairs
strolling the shadows beneath
the zigzag strings of incandescents.

No matter
the ride ends shortly

and everyone will be gone
before this hour passes.

Shirt-sleeved, rest
an arm on the silver bar and sit back.

Richard Pierce is an Assistant Professor of English at Waynesburg University. Born and raised in rural western New York, he earned his Ph.D. in creative writing and literature from Texas Tech University, where he was a Chancellor's Fellow. He also holds an M.A. from Ohio University and an M.F.A. from the University of Illinois. His poems have appeared in *Tar River Poetry, New South, Ninth Letter, Poet Lore, Relief,* and *Birmingham Poetry Review*. He has received scholarships to the Sewanee Writers' Conference and *Image Magazine's* GlenWest Workshop, and he has served as Managing Editor of *Iron Horse Literary Review* and Assistant Editor of *Ninth Letter*.

www.ingramcontent.com/pod-product-compliance
Lightning Source LLC
Chambersburg PA
CBHW030604020526
44112CB00048B/1244